PLAY IT
A PICTURE ALBUM

THE METROPOLITAN MUSEUM OF ART, NEW YORK

When rock and roll burst onto the scene in the 1950s, many observers thought it was just a fad. The first music created specifically for teenagers, it was denigrated by adults more accustomed to Frank Sinatra's smooth vocals and Benny Goodman's big-band swing. To them, rock and roll's driving beat was not only simplistic but downright dangerous; preachers professed that it was the devil's music, all too likely to stir the emotions and lead youngsters astray. But the baby-boom generation seized on rock and roll and didn't let go. It was more than a musical sensation; rock and roll was a social and generational phenomenon that became one of the most important artistic movements of the twentieth century. Its seismic influence reverberated across society, affecting fashion, youth culture, dance, sexuality, and free speech. It became a way of life.

Rock's outsize impact has been examined from almost every angle by writers, scholars, and curators, but never before has a presentation within an art museum been dedicated to the musical instruments that allowed for the creation of this powerful art form. The essential tools that inspire and make music, instruments are also the tangible artifacts of an ephemeral art. In rock and roll, their purpose is as visual as it is sonic: As physical objects, instruments can be appreciated not only for their craftsmanship and design but also for their contribution to the artist's

The destructive climax of the Who's set at the Monterey (Calif.) International Pop Festival, June 18, 1967

image; they are stand-ins for their players. They are, moreover, integral to stagecraft, even as the rock and roll concert has evolved to include theatrical staging and lighting, dancing, music, costumes, and occasionally even a narrative.

One of the first to exploit his instrument to such effect was singer, songwriter, and guitarist Chuck Berry, arguably the most important figure in rock and roll. His electric guitar solos in songs such as "Johnny B. Goode" (1958) revolutionized the music, making the instrument both the primary voice and a visual icon of rock and roll. Its amplification liberated players from having to stand behind a microphone; Berry capitalized upon this freedom by dancing while he played, unforgettably energizing his performances and thrilling audiences. Rock and roll guitarists ever since have made the most of the mobility afforded by electric guitars to perform similar antics. The introduction of the Fender Company's Precision model electric bass, which replaced the large upright acoustic bass, gave that instrument's players a similar range of motion. With the development of the keytar in the late 1970s, even keyboardists mimicked the striding performance style perfected by rock guitarists.

Though immobile, drum sets have also become part of the scenery and stagecraft of live performances, usually dominating the center of the stage. A notable example is Ringo Starr's drum set, raised on a platform behind his fellow Beatles during their performances on *The Ed Sullivan Show* in 1964. Later drummers adopted ever larger drum sets and imposing racks of equipment. Colossal drum sets used by musicians such as Alex Van Halen of Van Halen, John Bonham of Led Zeppelin, and Lars Ulrich of Metallica command the stage like monumental modernist sculptures. Keyboard rigs could also be configured for dramatic effect, especially the gigantic displays associated with progressive rock. The banks of electric organs and synthesizers that Rick Wakeman of Yes played

"Frying Pan" Electro Hawaiian guitar, Rickenbacker, ca. 1934. Designed for Hawaiian-style steel playing and released by 1932, the "Frying Pan" was the first commercially produced electric guitar.

resemble spaceship control panels from science-fiction movies; Keith Emerson of Emerson, Lake, and Palmer used a towering Moog modular synthesizer that could have come from the laboratory of a mad scientist. Lighting effects, lasers, and smoke machines augmented the spectacle.

Divorced from a performance context, musical instruments can be appreciated purely for their design. Many of the electric guitar models introduced in the 1950s and 1960s have become icons. The Fender Stratocaster, for example, designed by Leo Fender and his employees in 1954, features a sleek, asymmetrical silhouette with an ergonomic contour. A few years later, Gibson Guitar Corporation introduced the Flying V and Explorer, whose sharp-angled bodies were influenced by the space race and a cultural fascination with sci-fi visions of the future. Other firms, including Gretsch, Rickenbacker, and Danelectro, made guitars that featured unusual body shapes, incorporated plastics and metal in their construction, and were available in a host of bright, modern colors.

But while musical instruments may exemplify extraordinary design or be beautifully decorated, they are above all else tools for making music. The instruments themselves serve as inspiration for musicians. The squalling of the electric guitar — and the uncontrollable distortion and feedback that early amplifiers often produced — attracted pioneering rock and roll musicians and became hallmarks of the genre. Manufacturers producing a variety of guitar models with distinctive tones fostered creativity and experimentation. Drum sets, electric basses, and electric keyboards lent aggressive volume and tone to rock music, and synthesizers offered a host of otherworldly sounds. Together they defined the many strains of rock and roll.

Examining the instrumentation of the rock band and the way the instruments are used reveals the DNA of the music itself. Many of the instruments featured in early rock and roll were borrowed from genres

Keith Emerson performing with Emerson, Lake, and Palmer in Tuscaloosa, Ala., 1974. His rig includes a Moog modular synthesizer atop a Hammond organ, several other electronic keyboards, and customized speakers.

dominated by African American musicians. The saxophone and piano, for example, were originally played much as they were in R&B, jazz, jump blues, and boogie-woogie. The harmonica's use can be directly traced from black blues players to rock musicians such as Mick Jagger and Paul Butterfield. While the electric guitar was used across genres, including by such titans as Sister Rosetta Tharpe in gospel and Les Paul in jazz and pop, many rock and roll guitarists of the 1950s and 1960s picked up the instrument to emulate black electric-blues players like Muddy Waters and the three Kings (Albert, Freddie, and B. B.). Acoustic guitars, too, appeared across genres, but the large Martin and Gibson guitars Elvis Presley, the Everly Brothers, and other 1950s rock and rollers used to thump out rhythmic accompaniment can be traced to primarily white country-western influences like Jimmie Rodgers and Gene Autry.

Race and the racial tensions of midcentury American culture are in fact inextricable from rock and roll's history and development. The musical style was born in the segregated American South, where it was first played by primarily black ensembles. Radio exposed white audiences to performances by African American musicians of R&B, gospel, blues, and early rock and roll. To some white authorities, rock and roll was troublingly suggestive; their condemnation made the music even more attractive to white teenagers and reinforced its association with rebelliousness. White musicians and studios seized upon the music's popularity and swiftly brought it to the mass market; at the same time, many black musicians, including Little Richard and Chuck Berry, crossed over to capture mainstream audiences. Rock and roll was thereby a crucial part of changing attitudes concerning race across the country in the mid-twentieth century. Unfortunately, it wasn't nearly as progressive about women.

Rock and roll was for many years a boys' club. In the 1950s, 1960s, and even beyond, women in rock and roll bands were primarily limited

Carol Kaye, a prolific session musician, playing her Fender Precision bass in the studio, 1960s

to vocals. The notable exceptions, such as guitarists Wanda Jackson and Joni Mitchell and drummer Maureen Tucker from the Velvet Underground, prove the rule. The concept of the "guitar god" conflated hypersexualized male swagger, outrageous behavior, and virtuosic musical skill, narrowing the path for female musicians — especially at a time when women were expected to act like good girls. Later generations have made progress pushing back against this double standard; prime examples are guitarists Joan Jett, Courtney Love, P. J. Harvey, St. Vincent, and Carrie Brownstein. By 1994, when Brownstein cofounded her trio Sleater-Kinney, "a lot of those early battles . . . had already been fought," she said. "We were ultimately recognized as a band, not just as a female band, and that is a luxury that cannot be overstated."

Whether a guitar is being shredded by a Carrie Brownstein or a James Hetfield, the instrument itself is central to rock and roll's iconography as well as to its music. A perfect illustration regularly occurs at concerts featuring Don Felder, formerly lead guitarist of the Eagles. At some point in the performance, a guitar technician walks onto the stage carrying a white Gibson double-neck guitar, the mere sight of which causes the audience to go wild. It is a cue that Felder is about to play "Hotel California" (1976), the Eagles' biggest hit. The attendees' unrestrained, Pavlovian response to the Gibson has few parallels in music: no classical music audience applauds for a Stradivari violin; jazz connoisseurs don't give ovations to a Selmer saxophone. That is the unique power of the instruments of rock and roll.

Jack White, one of the most influential twenty-first-century rock guitarists, playing his Airline model Valco electric guitar with the White Stripes at the Bonnaroo Music and Arts Festival, Manchester, Tenn., June 16, 2007

Sister Rosetta Tharpe was anything but ordinary and plain. She was a powerful force of nature. A guitar-playin', singin' evangelist.

BOB DYLAN

Sister Rosetta Tharpe and Brownie McGhee perform a blues number on Granada Television's *Blues and Gospel Train*, recorded at the old Wilbraham Road railway station in Manchester, England, on May 7, 1964.

Chuck Berry duckwalking as he plays guitar at the TAMI Show, Santa Monica, Calif., October 1964

ES-350T archtop hollow-body electric guitar, Gibson, 1957. Chuck Berry used this guitar to record "Johnny B. Goode."

If you had tried to give rock and roll another name, you might call it Chuck Berry.

JOHN LENNON

> You're kind of [stuck] at a nine-foot plank and you've got to do something about it. So my thing was to leap on the piano, do handstands and wear clothes that would draw attention to me because that's the focus of two and a half hours.
>
> **ELTON JOHN**

Jerry Lee Lewis — one of rock and roll's first piano showmen — performs "Great Balls of Fire" with his band in the film *Jamboree*, 1957.

Baby grand piano, George Steck and Co., ca. 1955. Lewis kept and used this piano in his Memphis-area home for more than fifty years.

Bo Diddley with a version of his "Twang Machine," Norma-Jean "the Duchess" Wofford playing another custom-made guitar, and Jerome Green, ca. 1957

The "Twang Machine" electric guitar, Gretsch, ca. 1960

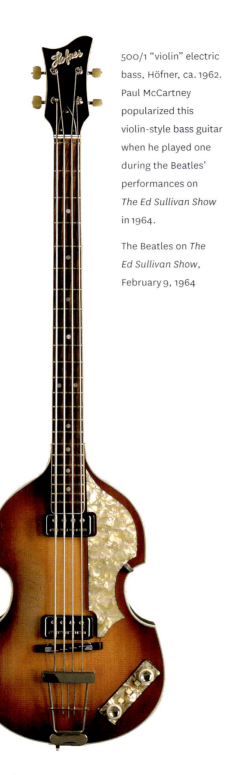

500/1 "violin" electric bass, Höfner, ca. 1962. Paul McCartney popularized this violin-style bass guitar when he played one during the Beatles' performances on *The Ed Sullivan Show* in 1964.

The Beatles on *The Ed Sullivan Show*, February 9, 1964.

Rickenbacker 325 twelve-string electric guitar, 1964. This guitar was specially made for John Lennon, who used it on the Beatles' first American tour in 1964.

Ringo's beat was heard around the world and he drew the spotlight toward the rock and roll drummer. From his matched-grip style to his pioneering use of staggered tom-tom fills, his influence in rock drumming was as important and widespread as Gene Krupa's had been in jazz.

MAX WEINBERG

Four-piece drum set with cymbals, Ludwig, 1963. After Ringo Starr played these drums with the Beatles on *Ed Sullivan* in 1964, the Ludwig factory had to go into round-the-clock production to meet the voracious demand for "Ringo" drum kits. In recognition, the company presented Starr with a gold-plated Ludwig snare drum.

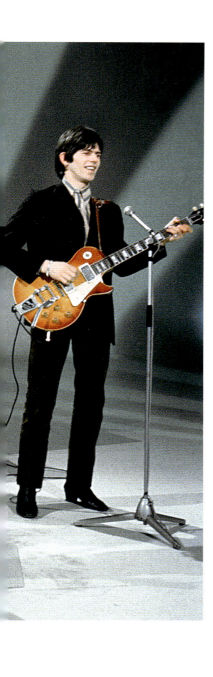

The Rolling Stones performing in 1964, featuring Keith Richards (near left) with his 1959 sunburst Les Paul Standard electric guitar (also shown at right)

Gibson's modernistic Flying V, now an icon of guitar design, did not find popular success for decades after its 1958 debut. This example from 1959 was used by Neil Young in the 1970s.

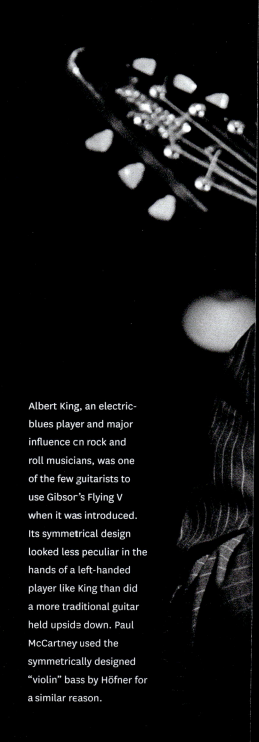

Albert King, an electric-blues player and major influence on rock and roll musicians, was one of the few guitarists to use Gibson's Flying V when it was introduced. Its symmetrical design looked less peculiar in the hands of a left-handed player like King than did a more traditional guitar held upside down. Paul McCartney used the symmetrically designed "violin" bass by Höfner for a similar reason.

Atmospheres are going to come through music because music is in a spiritual thing of its own.

JIMI HENDRIX

Jimi Hendrix solos above his head, setting new and subsequently oft-imitated standards for rock showmanship, 1967.

"Love Drops" Flying V electric guitar, Gibson, 1967. Painted and played by Jimi Hendrix, this guitar was later stripped down and repainted black. Eventually it was restored with Hendrix's design.

EDS-1275 double-neck electric guitar, Gibson, 1971. Jimmy Page used this guitar in live performances of "Stairway to Heaven" and other songs.

At every gig . . . there is the Clapton-idolising contingent who shout out things like "Give God a solo" or "We want more God."

NICK JONES, *MELODY MAKER*

Eric Clapton playing "Blackie," his 1956–57 Fender Stratocaster electric guitar, in a performance with Pete Townshend at the Rainbow Theatre, Finsbury Park, London, 1973

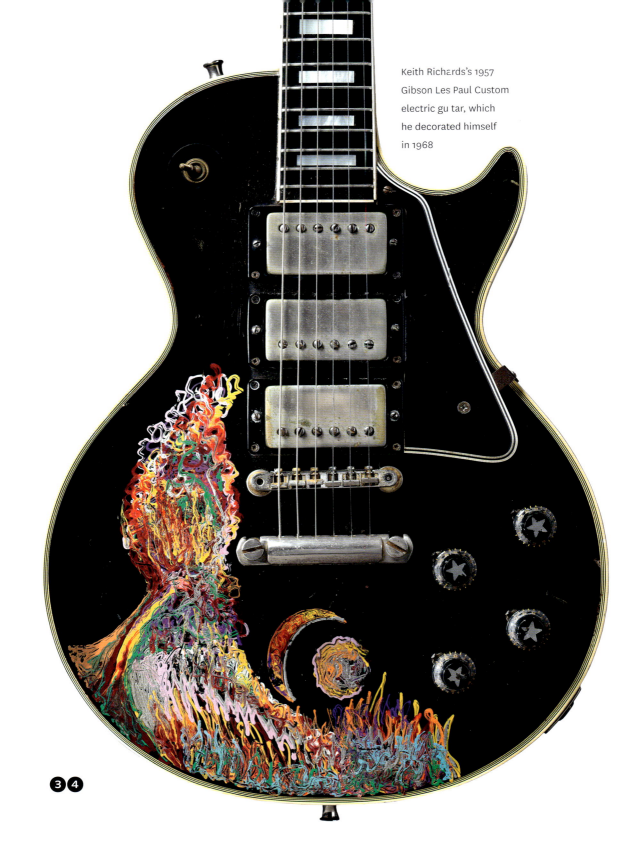

Keith Richards's 1957 Gibson Les Paul Custom electric guitar, which he decorated himself in 1968

Les Paul Special electric guitar, Gibson, 1961. This lavishly decorated, customized double-cutaway guitar was painted for Steve Miller by surfboard artist Bob Cantrell.

"Wolf" electric guitar, commissioned by Jerry Garcia from luthier Doug Irwin and completed in 1973

Garcia with "Wolf" at a Grateful Dead concert at the Uptown Theater in Chicago, November 18, 1978

Mark VI tenor saxophone, Henri Selmer Paris, 1967. Clarence Clemons used this Mark VI throughout his career with Bruce Springsteen and the E Street Band. The model is one of the most sought-after saxophones among jazz musicians.

With your first success, an image you'll be shadow-boxing with for the rest of your life embeds itself in the consciousness of your fans. You've left your fingerprints on your audience's imagination . . . and they stick.

BRUCE SPRINGSTEEN

Clemons and Springsteen in performance with the E Street Band, 1970s

"Punk Bass" custom FB4, Modulus, ca. 1998. Owned by Flea (shown playing it with the Red Hot Chili Peppers in 2002, opposite), this heavily decorated bass features carbon-fiber neck construction.

A master of developing a distinct, holistic identity via costumes, stagecraft, spectacle, and sheer musical talent, Lady Gaga performs with her crystal keytar during the Monster Ball tour, LG Arena, Birmingham, England, May 28, 2010.

St. Vincent signature electric guitar, Ernie Ball Music Man, 2017. St. Vincent designed this instrument to meet her ergonomic and stylistic needs.

St. Vincent performing with Dave Grohl and Krist Novoselic of Nirvana at the twenty-ninth annual Rock and Roll Hall of Fame Induction Ceremony at Barclays Center, Brooklyn, New York, April 10, 2014

We live Pop Art. I bang my guitar on my speaker because of the visual effect. . . . One gets a tremendous sound, and the effect is great.

PETE TOWNSHEND

Les Paul Deluxe electric guitar, Gibson, 1975. Pete Townshend had his tech number his guitars so he could differentiate their tunings onstage.

The text for this book was written by Jayson Kerr Dobney, Frederick P. Rose Curator in Charge of the Department of Musical Instruments at The Metropolitan Museum of Art, and Craig J. Inciardi, Curator and Director of Acquisitions at the Rock and Roll Hall of Fame, and was adapted from the catalogue published in conjunction with "Play It Loud: Instruments of Rock and Roll," on view at The Metropolitan Museum of Art, New York, from April 8 through October 1, 2019, and at the Rock and Roll Hall of Fame, Cleveland, from November 20, 2019, through September 13, 2020.

The exhibition is made possible by the John Pritzker Family Fund, the Estate of Ralph L. Riehle, the William Randolph Hearst Foundation, Diane Carol Brandt, the Paul L. Wattis Foundation, Kenneth and Anna Zankel, and the National Endowment for the Arts.

It is organized by The Metropolitan Museum of Art and the Rock and Roll Hall of Fame.

The exhibition catalogue was made possible by The Andrew W. Mellon Foundation, The Met's Friends of Musical Instruments: The Amati, Nion McEvoy, and Joseph O. Tobin II.

Published by The Metropolitan Museum of Art, New York
Mark Polizzotti, Publisher and Editor in Chief
Gwen Roginsky, Associate Publisher and General Manager
 of Publications
Peter Antony, Chief Production Manager
Michael Sittenfeld, Senior Managing Editor

Edited by Nancy E. Cohen
Designed by Susan Marsh
Production by Lauren Knighton
Image acquisitions and permissions by Jenn Sherman

Photographs on pages 1 and 46 are by Joseph Coscia Jr., Imaging Department, The Metropolitan Museum of Art. Additional photograph credits: Courtesy of Bob Bishop: 14; Photo by Clayton Call / Redferns: 39; CBS Photo Archive / Getty Images: 20–21 top; Everett Collection Inc. / Alamy Stock Photo: 16; Courtesy of Guernsey's, New York: 36; Courtesy of Julien's Auctions / Summer Evans: 22–23; Photo by Jeff Kravitz / FilmMagic for Superfly Presents: 10; Courtesy of Piyanun Margouleff: 20 left, 25 right, 26 left; Photo by Kevin Mazur / WireImage: 44–45 right; Image © Metropolitan Museum of Art: 5; Courtesy of Steve Miller: 35; © Museum of Pop Culture: 19; Photo by Paul Natkin / Getty Images: 37; Photo by Michael Ochs Archives / Getty Images: 9; Courtesy of Yoko Ono: 21 bottom; PA Images / Alamy Stock Photo: 40; Courtesy of Jimmy Page: 31; Pictorial Press Ltd. / Alamy Stock Photo: 15, 18, 24–25 left, 32; Photo by Michael Putland / Getty Images: 6; Courtesy of Keith Richards: front cover, 34; Courtesy of the Rock and Roll Hall of Fame: 17, 30, 38, 41; Photo by Paul Ryan / Michael Ochs Archives / Getty Images: 2; Courtesy of St. Vincent: 44 left; Photo by Peter Timm / Ullstein Bild via Getty Images: 29; Trinity Mirror / Mirrorpix / Alamy Stock Photo: 12–13; Wenn Ltd. / Alamy Stock Photo: 42–43; Photo by Kirk West / Getty Images: back cover; Photo by Baron Wolman / Getty Images: 26–27 right

Typeset in National and Tungsten
Printed on 150 gsm Perigord
Separations by Professional Graphics, Inc., Rockford, Illinois
Printing and binding coordinated by Ediciones El Viso, Madrid
Printed by Brizzolis, Madrid, and bound by Ramos, Madrid

Cover illustrations: front, Keith Richards's hand-painted 1957 Gibson Les Paul Custom electric guitar; back, the Grateful Dead and their immersive "Wall of Sound" P.A. system at the Iowa State Fair, Des Moines, June 16, 1974

Frontispiece: Eight-string custom electric bass with silver spiderweb inlays, which John Entwistle designed with Alembic, ca. 1976

The Metropolitan Museum of Art endeavors to respect copyright in a manner consistent with its nonprofit educational mission. If you believe any material has been included in this publication improperly, please contact the Publications and Editorial Department.

Copyright © 2019 by The Metropolitan Museum of Art, New York

FIRST PRINTING

All rights reserved. No part of this publication may be reproduced or transmitted in any form or by any means, electronic or mechanical, including photocopying, recording, or any information storage and retrieval system, without permission in writing from the publishers.

The Metropolitan Museum of Art
1000 Fifth Avenue
New York, New York 10028
metmuseum.org

Cataloguing-in-Publication Data is available from the Library of Congress.
ISBN 978-1-58839-699-0